waterways books

SUITCASE

releasing new voices, revealing new perspectives

SUITCASE

waterways
Printed and Bound in the United Kingdom

Published by waterways, 2004
www.waterways-publishing.com
an imprint of flipped eye publishing
All Rights Reserved

First Edition
Copyright © Roger Robinson 2004
Reprinted 2007

Cover Image & Design © Ninety, 2004

ISBN-10: 0-9542247-7-9
ISBN-13: 978-0-9542247-7-6

"....the glimpse given life, turned into something that illuminates the moment"

Raymond Carver

SUITCASE

for Kwame Dawes, Peter Kahn and Phyllis Robinson

Roger Robinson
2004

ACKNOWLEDGEMENTS

I would like to thank Isele Robinson, my beatiful wife Nicola Griffiths, Suzanne Alleyne, Bernadine Evaristo and Ruth Borthwick for their help while at Spread the Word, Colin Channer, Kwame Dawes, Ninety, Nii Ayikwei Parkes, Geraldine Collinge at Apples and Snakes, and members of the Poetry Kitchen - Jacob and Malika particularly.

SUITCASE

CONTENTS

I

Song for Angela

My mother is a twin,
or should I say my mother
is part of a twin.
My grandmother told me
that they used to sing together.
She showed me a picture
of them winning prizes.
What people didn't know
is that they actually
had the same voice, she said,
and together,
they had a haunting texture
that would impress the judges
time after time.

As a child
I remember sleepy nights
in small theatres,
where they'd raise
their voices in chorus,
their afros perfectly global,
framing their faces like halos.
Their dashiki robes,
like cloth equivalents
of the stained glass windows
of the Sistine chapel,
as they belted out
their folk tune chorus.

When I was a teen
one morning I saw them cooking

an Easter weekend brunch.
As they diced and chopped
the smell of fresh thyme
and baking fish
hung in the air like mist,
I heard them start a tune together in key,
without any signals,
not even a look,
their afros now straightened out
into razor sharp bobs,
falling at their cheeks
as thick and fluid as Indian ink,
their dashikis abandoned
for batik wraps, folk tunes replaced
by hymns with calypso flavour.
They sang their duet to god in unison
for three hours, till the food
was ready to be served.

I saw them sing again,
together in that room
when Angela,
my mother's twin,
her face serene
as a newborn baby's,
lay in bed;
my mother's hair cropped
short and grey with age;
Angela's hair short
through chemo
and grey with age;
holding my mother's hand,
saying she felt no pain

saying she had no regrets
saying goodbye to everyone.
Then they sang:
"Then sings my soul my saviour god to thee
How great thou art, how great thou art
Then sings my soul, my saviour god to thee
How great thou art, how..."
then she squeezed my mothers hand
stopping her short,
and my mother looked at her
and Angela whispered, she's *ready,*
and pushed her head back
into her pillow
as if to get comfy for her journey
as she smiled and closed her eyes.

Today, this Easter morning
my mother starts cooking brunch,
and she's trying to keep a tune
past the cracks in her throat.
Smiling through her tears
she stops; she starts again
trying to hold her tune
past the tears, palming them
off her cheeks, she stops.
She starts again, and I join in
to sing Angela's part.

The New Puppies

When I visit my mother at Christmas
she always has new puppies.
Brown and white furballs, with tiny slit eyes
short legs and floppy ears. They're like clones
of last year's puppies and the year before's.

Now I'm an adult; my age has bought rank.
I'm allowed to sit royally and shout
commands at my young cousins and stray kids
too poor to have a good Christmas elsewhere.
They shine my shoes and bring me orange juice.

They in turn try to get the puppies
to fetch thrown balls and twigs in the backyard,
but the puppies only respond to bowls of milk
and a tickled stomach, as they roll over
catatonic with the joy of touch.

At night I stay up late with my mother
making traditional Christmas snacks
as night rain hits the tin roof like applause.
She wakes each one of the seven children
individually at different times. She gives each one

a special snack and a hug and makes them swear
not to tell the others; so they all wake with the glow
of a favourite child. I ask her what has happened
to all the old puppies and she gives
various reasons like: a bigger dog killed them

or they ran away, or they were crushed
by a reversing car. She says this without
a dimming in her eyes, or a lilt of sorrow
in her voice, like someone used to losing
things and having them replaced.

Suitcase

My mother tells me that for years
she has kept a packed suitcase

in her car trunk, just in case
she had to leave urgently.

The square sky-blue leather suitcase
lay nudged against the spare wheel.

I ask what's inside? She unzips it,
and flips the top open.

There's a black and white picture
of my sister and I when we were

eight and six, wearing white,
matching vests and shorts,

my sister is crying and I
wear an afro with a side part.

There are four white Marks and Spencer,
size thirty two C bras, still in their box.

A smooth black leather copy of a New
Testament Bible, vacuum packed.

Two lemon-scented candles
and an orange torch light.

A yellowed birth certificate and a marriage
certificate slightly torn where it's creased.

An aquamarine toothbrush and one
dark maroon Fashion Fair lipstick.

A wooden hairbrush with stiff bristles.
An address book with her mother,

brother's and sister's addresses,
and numbers written in red.

Twenty white airmail envelopes
with red and blue striped borders.

And recycled brown writing paper
flecked with purple flowers petals.

This is all she needed.

Informers

She'd probably had a hard day at the clinic
with children screaming from the fear of injections.

So she wouldn't want to waste minutes of relaxing time
to find out who broke her favourite coffee cup.

So she'd wrap my father's scuffed leather belt firmly
around her knuckles and say to us that we'd be beat

to within an inch of our lives or until one
of us spoke up whichever would come first.

Then she'd quickly grab any one of us and raise
the belt strap threateningly, at which point we'd all

expose the guilty culprit with pointed fingers
who'd then get several belt straps around his thighs.

My mum was short and stocky and had tremendous
triceps that were a mixture of fat and muscle.

And when she beat, the hanging flesh would roll around
with the power of a crashing tsunami wave.

Then she'd confuse us all by saying we shouldn't be
sissy tell tales and give us each one strap of the belt.

Early Epitaph

1.

Daffodils highlight the slow sinking sun
as we travel by train to the cancer
clinic. Rural Germany holds answers
and beauty. The entire trip my mum
recommends dream pursuit for the young
and healthy. She tells me to take chances
and really live life. The sunlight dances
in the carriage. She looks outside and hums
a gospel tune. On the last note she lays
her head on the window. She falls asleep
and I'm wondering if this is my last
image of her alive, with bright bouquets
of flowers around her face. Her peace complete.
No dreams of missed love, she has let pass.

2.

At BadSteben station my mother says
that it is important to live your life
like you'd want to be thought of on your day
of burial. What would my death be like?
I think of what some will say when I'm dead,
that I was a man of plainspoken pride,
or that my ghosts slept fitfully in beds
of shallow graves. Here in this grave lies
a man who loved hard, and was loved hard back.
In his life kindness counted, a few words
of encouragement, or some idle chat
and gentle touch. This buried man preferred
the whisper of rain on the glassy lake,
and the arms of sunlight gilding his face.

Hug

He lay flat on the floor with his eyes open
but it was clear that no one was in.
Our local mechanic had become a shell
like one of the many rusted burnt out
cars that he'd work on in his garage.

He'd been like that for two days
from the moment he'd heard
that his father died from a heart
attack. His sister phoned my mother
because she was fluent in affairs of spirit.

I saw my mother kneel beside him.
She started chanting and rocking, to and fro
and with a breath, she pulled up
his limp torso, and placed his head
on her shoulder, her tiny arms

barely linked around the width
of his muscular back.
Onlookers might have thought
this woman grieving for a dead lover,
or perhaps a mother

trying to keep her son warm,
or that life was being squeezed
out of him. As she chanted,
rocked and rubbed, life
shimmered back. He began to blink.

And now
living so far away from her,
my head upon her shoulder, her
voice in my ear, tiny arms around me
squeezing life… A hug. A hug.

Churchgoing Momma

I've got paid tickets
to heaven. I won't let the
devil drag me down.

The Wedding Picture

I do not know any of these women,
these bridesmaids at my mother's wedding.

My mother knows just which beehive hairdo
ground her kneecaps away praying for her son

who everyone said was gay, even though he
swore to her that he was not, and she would

make the sign of the cross and drop
to her knees every time she thought about him.

My mother also knows which smile broke
down from too much alcohol and bad men,

who shaved off her hair and walked naked
and barefoot down Clapham High Street.

And mother knows which fuchsia satin dress
had been living with her man for fourteen years

and had two children and a house with him
'til he went away on holiday to Miami,

only to hear from a friend three weeks later
that he got married and he wasn't coming back

and that same woman took him back
when everyone abandoned him

because his body was so riddled with cancer
that he smelled like compost.

2

The Gift

When I rang you up to tell you
of my gift of fruit, a ripe mango,
you said that you weren't
really into the taste of them
and quickly moved the conversation
on to some film you enjoyed.
Perhaps I should have told you
how I braved the neighbours
sleeping dog and climbed up
the tree's creviced meld of branches.
Then the dog awoke, and I stayed
there amongst the smell
of ripe mangoes and wild flowers
watching the flags of everyday life
flutter on washing lines
under a scorching sun,
and watching a madman roasting
in the sun like an empty peanut shell
and mothers parting the wild growth
of their daughters' hair
like lush parcels of farmland,
until the dog drunk with heat
took to a second sleep.
Perhaps then you might have accepted
my gift, the mango with skin
smooth and unblemished
by ripeness, bird or stone
even if you didn't like it.

Riot

Her boyfriend rings at eight.
She talks about her day,
the loan refusal, the new shoes,
what she'll have for dinner.

And I lie in bed looking round
the room. The pale pink
ceramic Virgin Mary
on the windowsill,

the small red book of psalms
on the oak bedside table,
the dozen silver necklaces
slung over the iron bed post.

She puts the phone down
and says she can't afford
to leave him, as she turns on
the TV and comes to bed.

I roll her white cotton panties
down her legs and kiss her
inside her thighs. The newsman
announces a riot in Brixton.

We look out the window
and we don't see anything.
She pulls up her panties,
and we get our coats and walk

to the main road and see
a bus turned on its side
with one back wheel
still spinning.

And the chip shop is on fire
with a man and woman
sitting on the pavement,
with their heads in their hands.

Lab
(For Maria)

1

It was the year we used the biology lab. We entered to the gassy smell of the Bunsen burners, the anatomical charts and the lacquered, dark brown surface of the tables. The thing that I remember most is the row of jars, descending in height, that contained babies. Not dolls, or models, but real children, the colour of pickled onions slid into jars, like fish to be gazed at.

2

That year Mark told me that his girlfriend was pregnant, and that they wanted to use my house because both my parents worked. We left school at lunchtime to meet his girlfriend; by the time we got to my house she was wiping tears in her school shirt. I lit the kitchen stove and boiled some Guinness whilst Mark put the brown, twenty-dollar pill on the table. We all sat staring at it for ten silent minutes. She said she couldn't do it and he began to beg her to. I reheated the Guinness and brought it back to the table, and that time she drank it down and lay down in the bedroom. Mark and I tried to watch some TV. She screamed out and ran to the toilet. Mark grabbed my hand as she screamed for the next ten minutes then she stopped. She walked out dazed and stumbled to the couch.

3

I wiped the spilled sticky brown Guinness from the stove, scrubbed the bloodstains from the toilet bowl and changed the sheets soaked with sweat in the bedroom. After an hour they called a taxi. I looked at her through the tinted window. Crouched like a punished child on the back seat. The grey waxed shine of the car. Mark's worried eyes, the smell of the exhaust and the disappearing speck.

List

I faced the twelve names, written
in powder blue chalk capitals,
on the blackboard's far right.

My name was sixth, sandwiched
between Damon Beharry
and Barry J Kowlessar.

This was the list of virgins.
My dates had always ended
before joining, until the night

I recycled my best friend's lyrics
on a thirty year old woman.
She lived alone, four doors down,

and was friends with my mother.
I told her that I couldn't
stand being around her

without wanting to touch her.
The next day when my parents
left for work. I lay there

naked, nervous and inside her.
The day was hot, we looked
as if our bodies were sprayed,

and heat rose in waves
as if outside was melting.
When she left,

I lay there looking
up at a crack in the ceiling. Unsure
of how I was feeling.

The next day in school I wiped
my name from the virgin's list
and sat quietly at my desk

with a forced smile,
as the whole class stared
at the smudge where my name used to be.

UFOs

My first virtually real experience
was in my view finder when I was ten.

I flicked through pictures from National
Geographic and Richie Rich cartoons,

but then Bert, my next door neighbour
had secured a reel of naked women.

Sometimes I'd look at it in the house
while they all watched TV, they couldn't tell,

but most times I'd lie on my back at the end
of the garden with my magic binoculars

pointing to the sky for light, like someone
searching for UFOs, flicking through

woman after woman. One on a beach
holding a blue and white ball on her waist.

The other with, large, dark brown areolae.
There was another with a red cricket cap

with a bat in her hand and nothing else on.
After a few hours, I'd rise, and the grass

beneath me would be pressed down
to form a shape; the clear shape of a man.

Present

1
It was the Christmas of '74,
and all I wanted in the world

was the Six Million Dollar man
with the bionic eye .

2
Renault, was the guy who'd mow our lawn.
He asked mum for the rusty bike

that lay rotting in the garage,
as a Christmas present for his son.

Each evening Renault would scrape,
sand and coax the bike back from rust.

And he'd spray layer after layer
of candy red metallic paint.

3
Christmas morning I shredded the gift
paper and box to find small Steve Austin.

I looked through his bionic eye
which was really just a glass hole.

and after fifteen minutes he was buried
in the graveyard of old toys, the cupboard.

For the rest of that day I looked
through my window at Renault's kid

riding his bright red bike, and I wanted it
back. I wanted my old rusty bike back.

Class

The topic was housing.
My lecturer asked
"If you've been to public school
            stand"
Everyone stood but me.
He asked:
"If you live in a detached house
            stand"
 Nobody moves. I sink deeper.

He delights in this:
"Do you see how closely class
and housing intertwine.
Excellent. Everyone sit.
Robinson for the benefit
of the please tell us
about the tower block
you live in"

I rise, slow.

What do you want to know?
What do you want to know?

Do you want to know
about the toddler who lives
next door who screams
"mummy mummy" every night
for an hour through the postal
flap in the door as it echoes

down the acoustics of the hall
'cause his mother can't afford a sitter
flipping burgers, in Mc Slavery
or about the baby that fell
from the tenth floor window
just in front of all the children
playing downstairs.

One of the kids
I hear she was only eleven years old
took off her coat,
covered the baby and knelt down
to make an arc
with her body over it,
while the others tried to hold
the mother back from the shock
of seeing her child like smashed pulp.
Is that what you want to know?
Or do you want to know
about summer Sunday mornings
when I lean my head out
my eighth floor window
and see a whole tribe of women
aunts, nieces mothers – daughters
on their way to church
all in pastel green dresses
because it's cheaper
to buy a whole roll of cloth
than to buy a yard.

and one house upstairs
is playing reggae
and another downstairs
is playing soca
so what I'm hearing
is some perfect fusion.
Somebody knocks on my door
and it's a woman who's trying
to get her O levels in English
and maths, wondering
if I could help her
from time to time
because she heard
that I'm at University.

The Ex Picture

On that murky midwinter day
your girlfriend walks slowly
towards you, brandishing
a picture of your ex-girlfriend,

asking why you still kept
her tucked between
your important documents,
in the cracked leather holdall,

perched neatly between your birth
certificate and your passport.
You try to pretend that you didn't
know where she found it.

She asks you if you're still
in love with her, and you dismiss
her with a blunt "Of course not!"
"Prove it then," she says. "Tear it up."

You hold her in your hands
slowly rip through, twice,
throw it in the bin
and continue to wash the dishes.

Was it then that you learned
to sacrifice your feelings for someone
else's? Did you begin to know
how being tested felt? If you spoke

up would she hear sadness?
At certain angles the light
shimmering off the tape,
still obscures her face.

Confessional

We had months of preparation,
but at age ten we could never
really understand how it would be
confessing your sins to someone.

In my grey shorts, starched
white shirt and black shoes buffed
to shine, I knelt between the pews
and mimed the words to prayers I forgot.

As we lined up for the confession booth,
I looked back at my parents
who looked proud and concerned
as if I were being sent off to war.

The ornately carved wooden booth
smelled like shoe polish. I could see, through
the screen, the Irish priest's scowling silhouette
as he asked if I'd any sins to confess.

I thought for a while and said "No."
He said "Are you sure? Think about it."
I searched every crevice of my brain
"Sorry, I have no sins to confess."

His voice rose to shouting.
"We are all sinners and you must
confess for forgiveness. Have you had
any unclean thoughts?"

Even though I hadn't, I thought
that I'd better tell him what he wanted to hear.
"Uuuuhhh Yes I've had unclean thoughts"
He asked if I'd lied or stolen.

"Uuhhh. Yes I've lied and I've stolen."
This is how I came to invent
an incredible resumé of sins
complete with minor details.

The bigger the sin the more
he nodded his head and stroked
his chin. He told me to recite
twenty Hail Marys.

Western

We talked most evenings for two weeks
and she suggested that we should go
to the movies on that weekend.

I wanted to take her to see something
good, so I looked through the cinema
listings and saw *Enter the Dragon*

with Bruce Lee. This was perfect:
I was waiting for weeks for this film.
It felt like I was seeing a kung fu film

for the very first time again.
The lights dimmed and flickered
and she slid her hands into mine.

Bruce Lee was kicking and fighting
his hand speed was blurring
he shuffled around like Muhammad Ali.

His skin was paper thin, you could see
every muscle and his nunchakus
were like arm extensions.

Then I felt a kiss on my neck
coming slowly round my cheek
to my lips. I thought, "Come on

you must be kidding – this is Bruce Lee;
look around, nobody else is kissing.
If I wanted this I would have taken you

to see some old Western."

Lost Fight

Bruised skin stretched smoothly
over a structural bulge of blood vessels.
Less than the fleshy thickness of a scar
but more than the flushing blood of fear
or embarrassment. Still a tender and delicate
epaulette of trauma, a badge proclaiming to all
that without breaking skin or bone
a blunt and heavy blow has been absorbed.
And pain's floret shall eventually pass,
its mauve hue just a measure of time.

Mistake

"I like making
 love to you,"
I said.

She misheard
and said,

"I think
 I'm in love
 with you
 too."

3

Mattress

I was just fourteen years old
when my father pissed the bed.
The powder blue striped mattress
with white stiff nylon piping,
leaned against the outside wall,
the wind wafting the golden
smell of urine through the yard.
The sun shined on the pale stain
in the vague shape of Texas.
Dad skulked around avoiding
all our eyes, then he drove off.
Mum filled a black plastic bucket
with steaming soapy water
and told me in a low voice
that he was under some stress
at work. She dipped the hard
bristled brush in the bucket
and tried to scrub out the stain.

Beached

My father would burst in our room
at six am shouting "This is not a holiday
camp wake up, we're going to the beach!"
He'd rip the covers off my sister and I
and shout "The car leaves in fifteen minutes!"

The three-hour drive to Maracas beach
smelled like the stewed chicken
in the trunk, which gave way
to the taste of salt water mist on our lips
and the smell of fresh forest leaves.

My sister and I would always dig
a large hole in the sand, with our hands
shaped like ladles. We'd dig until blood
rose in our nails, put our father in
and cover him in sand, leaving his head out.

We'd run into the sea and look
at him. His head like a dot
on brown paper. We'd shout
to him to come in the sea,
and he'd shout that he was stuck.

Twenty years later I talk
to my sister on the phone;
she hasn't heard from him either.
She hopes the next time we see him
won't be to lower him in the ground.

Knowledge and Prayers

There was the time when my mother beat us
with a curtain cord slicing wails in our skin

and my father ran out the house crying.
I heard that when he was young his father

made him boil his belt before being beaten
with the belt buckle-side. Once his father

beat him on his back till his spine was bruised
and he couldn't walk for thirteen days.

Another time he was put in a corner
to kneel with his hands outstretched in the air.

His father left him there for an hour
and then he placed an encyclopaedia

in his outstretched hands, and left him there
for another hour. Then he added

a bible, and left him there, whilst his brothers
were sent to bed. They left him there

overnight.

Sleep

It becomes clear to you
the night your father asks you
to wake him up to see
his favourite film on TV,
and despite cups of coffee
bright lights and company
he is asleep
with his dark rimmed glasses
tilted on his face before
the opening credits.

And there
hearing the drag of his snore
and watching the uncomfortably
crooked angle of his neck,
you see him at nineteen,
taking care of his four brothers
and one sister and studying
for a scholarship while working
nights pushing dead bodies
at the local morgue, and he's tired
but he can't stop because he'll
be the first in their family
to go to university and he can't
let them down.

At twenty-one
he's in class at Sterling University
wondering if he can afford the batteries
for his warehouseman's torch
so he can study on the job tonight.
Nobody told him Scotland
would be this cold, and it's

so lonely sometimes but he
has to pass these exams
or he'll be out.

At twenty-two, you're born.
Your mother works the night shift
at the hospital, and he tries to read
between your two a.m. squeals
and he picks you up
in the hand not holding the book
and smiles and rocks you to sleep.

Twenty-five now,
and working late five nights a week
trying to snatch a few promotions,
and somehow he thought
it might be a bit easier with his degree,
and he really needs
to move his wife and kids
into a place of their own.

And for the next twenty years
he battles on his job every day
just so you could be comfortable
and have the space to be what you want.

And then you know
that he's never had much time for this
for rest, for sleep.
You prop his head with a pillow,
gingerly pull off his glasses
and stare at him
snoring, loudly,
beautifully.

Bat

One night I saw my father fight.
He unsheathed his cricket bat,
and charged out the front door

into the night, after a drug
peddler who threatened to molest
my younger sister. I was ten

and knew to stand a safe distance
away. I saw his silhouette
against the street lamp's pale white glow,

wielding his bat with righteous rage
'til the man was down. My father walked
back to the house tapping the smooth

open face of the bat against the meat
of his right thigh. He pulled a chair to the front
door and sat silently with the bat

on his left shoulder like a king.
My father, on his throne,
scanning the night for danger to his clan.

Wagon

The bank okayed the loan,
and my father bought the golden
brown Vauxhall station wagon

complete with am fm radio
stereo cassette player, shatterproof
windows and tanned leather seats.

On Saturdays he cleaned it
with a steaming bucket of bubbles
and a yellow chamois cloth.

I'd sit inside and see the world
through soap streaks and splashes,
watch layers of water slide

down the windscreen like a silk dress
down a woman's curves.
He'd shine it with a slow caress

'til the car caught the sun's glare,
'til he could see himself in it.
He'd scrub the tyres black before

he'd flip open the hood to check the oil
and water. Guys would drift
into our driveway to talk cars.

Amidst the waxy smell of polish
detergent and oil, they'd nod
over the exhaust manifold.

On Sundays he'd teach me
to drive. I was nine and I'd sit
on his lap to see over the steering.

I could feel the twitching of his thigh
muscles as he'd press his feet down
on the pedals. I'd turn the key

and hear the cough and sputter
of the engine. We'd circle the block
a few times with my tiny hand

on top of his changing gears,
soul music blaring from the speakers
and turning each corner slowly.

Later that year the oil company
laid him off and the bank
took the car back.

He rolled up the left leg
of his khakis and rode
a bike to his new job.

Leather and Vinegar

When my mother was away
my father would bring home
a thick cut of lean pink beef
wrapped snugly in brown paper
tied in a bow with twine,
and a corked emerald green
bottle of mid-priced Claret.
He'd take off his dark blue jacket
and tie whilst heading for the kitchen
as he rolled up his sleeves,
to make his favourite dish.
Beef Stroganoff.
He'd use every silver pot,
blackened pan and kitchen utensil,
taking extra care to measure
every ingredient to the ounce.
After stirring he'd always
bang the spoon a few times
on the edge of the pot
like some gamelan player
looking for a new tune.
Thirty years later as I cook
steamed vegetables and rice
for my mother I tell her
that I could never let him
know that at its best it tasted
like leather soaked in vinegar.

4

Stitch

I remember when Uncle Ken,
made ten graduation dresses
in one weekend, with cloth shapes
at his feet like a giant jigsaw.

He'd rethread his needle staring
at the sewing machine with his face
lit by the reading lamp followed
by the Singer's grinding drone.

From the kitchen I could hear
his giant scissors' snipping click
and the rustle of dress blueprints
stuck to the wall with masking tape

like ghostly women waltzing
above his shoulders. My job
was to dish the family gossip
and to make mud thick coffee.

And the cat would brush
against his shins, purr,
jump onto his lap
and curl up while he worked,

inserting the needle
at the back of cut cloth—
and drawn with a jerk
so tight as not to break.

The power of every stitch
confined to itself ;—
each placed as to preserve
the unbroken chain
behind.

He wore flowered shirts with platformed Converse trainers,
and dark brown corduroy flares that spread so wide
that it never looked like he walked. He just floated
everywhere. He used to play on the basketball
court, dribbling the ball between his legs
faking on one side and driving on the other.
Floating over tall men to stuff the ball in
the net. Always smirking as he leisurely jogged
up court to defend. His afro was always picked
and patted round, like a black space helmet.
He owned a stacked wall of eight-track soul love
ballads. He had no job, yet he always had money.
He never cleaned up, yet his house was spotless.
He never went shopping but his fridge was full.
My uncle was a player a Mac, a hustler, a Romeo
gigolo and ladies man. In nineteen seventy-nine
Trinidad won the Netball World Championships
and my uncle was sleeping with the entire
starting team, one substitute, an assistant coach
and a manager. All of these women were glorious
beauties smelling of Afrosheen and cocoa butter.
He'd lead each one into his bedroom and push in
an eight-track soul tape. Below his door I'd see
the glow of his red bulb with wisps of coconut
incense mixed in with the pungent smell of weed smoke.
And when they left they seemed slightly dazed and happy.
So this is a tribute to my Uncle Adrian, the player.

Her Thirtieth Year

The summer she turned twenty
we were liquid with heat.

We sat on the back door step
sipping cherry Kool-Aid

and watching the stained glass wings
of butterflies dart between dandelions.

She'd talk – with red lips and tongue
– of epics she'd write, awards

she'd collect at age thirty
and about when she was young.

She'd feed grass to caterpillars
till they sprouted wings and flew

and at night we'd make love with open
windows billowing the lace curtains.

Today would be her thirtieth year.
No longer dizzy with the warmth of dreams

I hear she cleans offices at night
somewhere in Manhattan.

Stephanie

His name was Stephen
though he answered to Stephanie.
At school we all wanted
to be doctors, lawyers, economists,
and even playwrights,

but he was the only student
at Naparima College Boys School
who wanted to be a make-up artist.
We didn't know what a make-up
artist was, but we assumed

it was a fancy job to do
with those foreign fashion magazines
that he'd flick through at lunch time.
Everybody knew Stephanie's
loud voice and quick humour.

And we all remember the day he began
wearing the spangling black boob-tube
under his flimsy white cotton school shirt.
At recess he'd undo a few buttons

to reveal his sparkle like a woman

showing cleavage. We were surprised
but not shocked. It was just Stephanie
being himself. And the year he came
to the school bazaar in wide black flares,

high-heeled slippers, full make-up
with hanging silver earrings
and the black sequined boob-tube,
we were surprised and amused,
but not shocked.

But when some girl shouted
"Who is this fool?" and he spun
round and shouted,
"This fool fucked your father!"
 Then we were shocked.

Ude

On the Underground
he asked if I'd sign his petition.
He, dressed in dazzling white sneakers
with three blood red stripes,

bare mask of a face
with eye-like nostrils.
What's it for? I asked.
"The police killed my father"
his eyes being the only crack
in the emotional dam of his face.

He handed me a pamphlet
and moved down the speeding train.
As I watched him gather names,
his broad shoulders swaying
like a sailor on deck during a storm,
I was reminded of a time
it seemed my father might die;
a simple peanut lodged in his throat
making him a helpless mound
of choking bones and flesh
on the kitchen floor.

My mother screamed
"Hurry Roger get the doctor!"
who lived next door.

In a panicked confusion
I ran downstairs

past the doctor's house,
straight up our tributary road
and up the hard shoulder
of the main highway.

All about me
were the florescent random drift
of fireflies and the crunching
rhythm of gravel beneath my shoes.

I walked as if I was leading
a procession, walked
mumbling prayers to clouds, walked
'cause I was too afraid
to go back and find him dead.

I glanced at Ude again
standing by the train doors
set adrift in the rush hour crowd
clutching a handful of strangers.

Virgin Island

She was nineteen caramel-coloured, thick-lipped,
and tall with curly hair that grazed her shoulders.

She had eyes that sloped up from her cheekbones.
Everyone wanted her, and she famously

rejected most of the guys in the area,
which earned her the nickname of Virgin Island.

The rumour was that her parents sent her here
because of some trouble that she got into.

She wanted to go to New York to be famous
in cinema, but her parents were too poor.

Her aunt, on holiday from New York, left her
a Big Apple diary and promised that if she raised

the plane fare, she could come and stay with her.
That was when she became the local bookie

for the 'whe whe' gambling ring. This was a form
of gambling based on dreams. Every day she'd miss

secretarial college and walk from house
to house and people would tell her their dreams.

So if someone dreamed about a big new house
that would be the number eight. If someone dreamed

of a bird that would be the number sixteen.

She'd take money, write the dream digits in

her Big Apple diary, take the cash
to the house where the numbers would be played,

and then she would be paid. This is how she thought
she'd make enough money to buy her ticket.

But she didn't know that the police had her
under surveillance. And on the day she saved

enough money for her ticket she was walking
to the travel shop when the police swooped down.

She tried to explain "No No this is not...New
York...money betting... it ain't...dreams... this is mine"

They took her diary full of dreams and her
two thousand dollars and she was arrested.

On the cell's cold grey slate she thought about New York
and she thought, and she thought and she thought.

Mango Juice

Trinidad is...

The green cat's eye
of the last marble left
from the two bulging pockets
that I win from my schoolfriend
Junior. As I slam his last
remaining marble
from the chalk circle
with a running start
he kicks me in the balls.
All week I stay home
with an ice pack on my balls
and all my mother's friends
visit asking me if my balls
are feeling any better?

Trinidad is....

The bead of sticky mango juice
running down my bony wrists.
And it's the Indian girl next door
who wears the same two dresses
all year round. She gives me a ripe
mango plumped to sweetness
once a week. She never talks
she just gives me the mango
and sits in the yard
with a goofy smile watching
me as I eat it, and then she leaves.
If she's trying to get me

to like her I can tell you right
now, it's working.

Trinidad is…

The first drop of warm rain
in the wet season.
And all the young kids run
out into the street
in their Jockey shorts
with a bar of soap
for a rain bath.

It's nights so warm
you feel you could reach up
and pluck the diamante stars
from the black velvet sky.
It's where I was, where I am
and where I'm going.
It's the knot in my throat
when I had to leave.

Conversion

Over dinner mum remembers
that I was six when we moved
back to Trinidad.

She said people would ask
my name and I would say
"Hhrroaja Hrrroabinsin"

and people would chuckle
at the black boy
with the Scottish accent.

One day she woke
to see me in the bedroom
mirror in blue y-fronts,

practising the accent
with full hand and facial
gestures. First in Scottish:

"Lukeit theis evrybuddy"
and then the conversion:
"All of allyuh, check dis out nuh."

Master

If I got through my times table
my teacher took me to kung fu films.
He had thick spectacles that looked
like the bottoms of whisky glasses.
Good teachers had one pen clipped
to their pocket. He had five.

At the first kung fu film I saw
the cinema crackled with excitement.
The only films I'd seen were Snow White
and Cinderella. There were no kids
or women as I rocked back to watch.
The Golden Harvest symbol glowed

and cut straight to the film. All the actors
were Chinese. A young woman served tea
to a restaurant full of men. Then one old man
grabbed her leg and she smashed the teapot
in his face. His friend jumped up and she
side-kicked him in the chest, into a pole.

I looked to my teacher to explain what kind of film
this was, but he was too wrapped up in the fighting
to notice me. He was shadowboxing in his seat.
There were people all down the aisles practicing
each move they saw in the film. The whole place

was jabbing and ducking. I can't recall the story
but even at that age I knew the plot was rubbish.
That wasn't the point; people being killed
in hand-to-hand combat was what we were there for.
As we left and the glare of the evening sun gilded
my face, I felt different, and my teacher knew.

I've seen you slowly steer
away from distractions to
your faith in God and people. It's kept you right
where you want to be, dodging the rain
keeping dry, but even when your heart is stretched
your work continues on.

Now it seems you are moving on,
as you fold and file your world into stark, austere
essentials. You plan everything and leave mistakes to
fate. Minimal life gives minimal worry. You've stretched
thoughts, kept your head right,
and listened to Ella's singing, like gentle rain.

And what you heard, from your people, made tears rain,
streaming wet on
your cheeks, but you knew it was a rite
of sadness, and even as you stared
outside your window and your view stretched
for miles, you knew that storms pass, but not sure where to.

You've forgiven so many too
and you've pulled in your reins
of anger so tight they've stretched
with the strain, but you carry on
with life, ignoring the stare
of people who don't think forgiveness is your right.

I'm not the writer, you are. You write

the truth in e-mails and essays to
friends and colleagues. Unlike you I never stare
into truth's bright glare. I only remove my shades when rain
falls, or at night – when lights aren't on;
I prefer my truths slightly stretched.

Your two hands remain outstretched
on the right
to your faith that supports you, and on
the left to
your friends, who you support, sheltering them from rain
and jealous stares.

My faith in you cannot be stretched. It's far too
strong. We ignore the rain
clouds. With you on the left and me on the right, we'll climb love's stairs.

Ticket

Long before Leticia left for New York
she was telling us how much she'd miss us.
She lived at the top of our road
in a rickety wooden house that leaned.

Her mother would borrow cups
of rice and sugar from neighbours
so no one took her New York talk seriously,
till the year she stopped kissing

the boys from the street. She could be seen
late at night giggling into the window
of a white Mercedes Benz. The last we heard
she was raising money for her sister's ticket

in the navy blue BMW
and the bottle green Jaguar with silver hubcaps.
We heard she touched down at JFK
a month later. We heard that she lied

to all three of them that she was pregnant
and needed money for an expensive abortion.
One abortion cost paid for her one-way ticket
and the rest went to her New York settling-in fund.

Wail

1

My first memory of my cousin was Christmas of 1970. He was ten and I was eight. His parents dropped him off on Christmas eve, and boy was he pissed. He knew he wouldn't be seeing them again. At night I could hear him sniffling into his pillow and when I asked him if he was alright, he'd snarl like an injured dog. "Fuck off you better stay the fuck away from me you fat little shit. I'm warning you don't even come near me you tub of lard. Don't even look at me. You better stay on your side of the room or else I swear to go I'll kill you."

2

I felt sorry for him all the same even though I was the one who should be pissed because he was sharing my room. I understood that this kind of thing was happening a lot now. If your parents didn't have a job in the Texaco oil refinery then it was hard. Lots of people were leaving Trinidad to find work as apple pickers in Canada, on the Underground in London, as nurses in New York. When we all sat for Christmas dinner that year we let him eat from a tray in the bedroom whilst we looked at each other shuffling our turkey around listening to him wail.

3

By the following Easter my father was packing his bags to look for labouring work in New York. He was leaving on Easter Sunday on a cheap ticket. My cousin and I ate our Easter dinner and we could hear my mother in the bedroom wailing. We took our dinner in there and watched her body shake with sobs, so wrapped up in her sadness she didn't even notice us. When she did see us she smiled and said "Don't worry boys I'm fine" and dabbed her tears with sleeves then said "Don't worry boys I'm fine, I'm right as rain, Happy Easter boys give me a hug." And we felt her body stutter.

She walks and golden
petals weave a carpet of
light. I fall for her.

Unseen

At the station, I see the blind
man reach for his wife.
He touches her face
with his open palm

and slides his fingers
slowly down to her lips,
as he leans over and kisses
where his fingertips touch.

What an Ex-girlfriend said after
a Love Poem at a reading.

Your poems that talk of honeyed winds
blowing round the room are blatant lies!

I was there. What's this shit about sucking
moons from my mouth? Sentimental fool!

Where's the part when I made you beg
to lick me like a puppy lapping milk?

Where's the part when I clawed your back
and the blood bubbled out hot and sticky like tar?

5

Uncle Robert's Letter To My Father

1.

Remember those skinny kids?
The ones we played cricket with,
all dressed in second hand clothes
and knees sticking out like bolts.
I remember each night they'd stoop
like Praying Mantis in the dark outside
the gate to watch our TV. Each night
you'd angle it in their direction and raise
the volume, and every night Ma
would shout "Nolan that TV's too loud,"
and you'd say "It ain't loud Ma,"
then she'd continue reading her bible
in the kitchen. Sometimes a show
would come on that made them forget
themselves, and a chorus of laughter
would bring Ma out looking over
her glasses and they'd scatter.
Ma would walk back with a smirk,
and we'd see their moonlit shoulders
jostling for space. Do you remember
what they called it? The movie house,
remember? They called it the movie house.

2.

I'll never forget the times
we'd play cricket in the road
with your sponge ball and wood bat.
When it was my turn to bat,
if I got out, you would say
I could have another try.

If anyone objected
you'd stick out your chest and say
"This is my bat and my ball.
If he can't bat one more time
then I'm taking my ball and bat
and the game will be over."
You eyeballed each of them
and sealed it by declaring
if there were more objections
there'd be no more movie house.
Those kids couldn't get angry.
I used to feel so special.
If you didn't help me out
I would hardly have a chance
'cause I was crap at cricket.
One time Mama heard your threats
and sent you to your room,
but I snatched the bat and ball.
When you leave, the game's over.

3.

I'd feel like we were a team,
like when "Bigfoot" stole my watch.
He was so big, six-foot-four,
two hundred pounds at fifteen.
When I said he took the watch
you didn't even say a word,
you stormed out looking for him
and when you found him you looked
up at him and told him to
"give the watch back now or else"
you'd have to take it back.

He said that it was his watch.
You looked at the growing crowd
and told him his mom must have
fucked a gorilla for him
to be so ugly and stupid.
I thought you'd lost your damned mind;
the watch wasn't worth being killed.
He started swinging wildly,
if just one of those punches
connected you'd have brain damage,
but you ducked and weaved each one
and, as soon as he gasped for breath,
you zoomed in with three punches
BAM! BAM! BAM! to his forehead.
You ripped the watch from his wrist
standing over him shouting:
"Nobody fucks with my brother!"
As we left I thought that you
were a black superhero,
like some kind of Black Batman
and I was a Black Robin.
I felt like with you by my side
there was nothing we couldn't do.

4.

When we were in Sixth Form,
on that day you saw me kiss
that boy behind the toilet,
you looked so disappointed.
I didn't want you to find out,
at least not in that way.
I always thought I'd sit you down

and come out to you alone
and you'd put your hand on mine
and say everything's all right
and that we'll always be a team.
I guess not everything goes
exactly how you want it.
You didn't talk to me for weeks
even though a friend told me
that your friends called me gayboy
and you said nobody calls
"my little brother a gayboy"
and you'd personally beat
anyone who even tries.
Is that true? I'm not surprised.
Even though we didn't talk
I knew you'd stand up for me.
To this day that's how I feel:
still hoping that you're cursing
someone out, defending me,
ready to fight if need be.

5.

Mama found out and got mad.
She sent you to uncle George.
It was terrible Ronald.
She just lit a white candle
in the corner of her room
and sat rocking her chair,
fingering her rosary
thumbing pages of her bible
for six straight days with no sleep.

Mama wasn't eating
she only drank water.
She wouldn't even look at me.
Everytime I'd ask something
she'd just say "Lawd give me strength!"
On the seventh day you came back
and she sent you to your room.
That night a bunch of church elders,
Pastor Thomas and all our aunts
descended on our house
and grabbed me up from the couch.
I couldn't escape. They held down
my arms and my legs and started
sprinkling water in my face.
Then the pastor starts squeezing
my head and starts to shout:
"Laawwd cast this satanic spirit
of homosexuality
out your son, Demon be gone!"
I'm sure you heard it from your room.
They were shouting and singing,
trying to cast this so-called demon
from me. I'd struggle to break free
and they'd start saying stupid shit like:
"Can you see brothers and sisters,
see Satan's power struggling!"
And when Mama shouted to you
to come from your room to help
hold me down, you didn't come out.
When I screamed out "Rooonaalld,
Rooonaalld help me," you came out though.
You stood there and looked at me
and your eyes told me that you

were on my side, that you were there
for me and I felt relaxed
as I looked in your eyes. The whole
time they were carrying on
I just kept looking at you
and I just felt very safe.
If you wasn't there for me
I'm sure I'd have killed myself.
And when they stopped and I stood
catching my breath with my hand
on your shoulder facing them
and I said that "I have loved men
ever since I was six years old
and I'll love men till I die,"
Ronald that was all I could do
to keep some of my self respect.
The humiliation of flesh
and blood thinking you're a demon
and all for what? Because I love
men? I looked at each of them
and saw no love in their hearts.
You know what hurt me the most?
It's when Mama said she had one son.
That hurt Ronald, that really hurt.
I knew then it was time to leave.
When I went to my room
to pack you just sat there with me
not even saying anything,
just being there. I've never told
you this, but you being there
and walking me to the gate,
past all of those lunatics,
was so important to me.
I think for the first and last time

we really hugged, even though you
said nothing I felt you man.
As I walked off I looked back
and saw you watching me leave.
I believe that's the last time
we saw each other Ronald.
About fifteen years ago now.

6.

I'll tell you a secret though
because even when I left
that day in a way I was still
with you. When you became
a big cricket star, my boyfriend
and I, we were there looking on
from the stands at all your games.
We never missed a match.
We saw every boundary,
every four that skidded past
the fielders' reach. Every six
that you lobbed like a grenade
that landed with an explosion
of cheers from the crowd.
And when you played your first game
for Trinidad and you scored
that century, I was jumping
up and down in the pavilion
with the crowd. I was like a madman
shouting "That's my brother boy!
That's my brother. We have the same blood,
the same blood!" As you raised your bat,

man I cried, I was so happy.
You didn't know that did you?
I was so proud of you, so proud.
Soon after that being gay
in Trinidad became dangerous.
Too much hate to be me;
that's why I left for England
so that I could be myself
and not go completely insane.
I'd rather face the cold grey rain
than spend my life pretending
for everyone else's comfort.
I just thought that you should know
how important you were to me
during that entire time.
Without you I might not have made
it through those ordeals alive.

7.

Anyway enough of the good
old days. So you're all right though?
Life, love and work going well?
It's winter here and the leafless
trees stand embarrassed and still.
The ground has tainted the virgin
snow to sludge. The clouds
are vaporous wisps. And the light
of the day is grey, the curtains
are still. I'm not doing so well
Ronald. A year ago a small bruise

on the inside of my arm
became a burgundy stain
so I had myself tested.
It was the worst three-week wait.
It felt like it took fifteen years.
The tests came back positive:
I kind of already knew.
The good news is that my partner
of four years, Tom, is negative
and he's with me loving me
twenty four hours a day.
Sometimes Ronald I think
that if he wasn't here with me
would I really die alone.
He's trying his best to be strong
but I worry about him.
One day the pain was too much
and he came back from the store
and asked if I was all right.
I answered with my back turned
in the best happy voice I could,
saying everything is just fine.
He walked around and saw my face
and took off his shirt and pants
climbed into bed and put his arms
around me and sang all his
favourite love tunes all night.
I'm getting worse, Ronald,
the last two weeks I've lost
ten pounds; I can't even hold
down tablets far less for food.
At night, sometimes I sweat so much

the mattress is soaked right through.
I'm so frightened Ronald.
I'd give any thing to have you
here with me like we were
back in the old days you and me
against anything. Drop me a line
or something. We're still a team
right? Just like back in the old days
right? Write to me and don't forget
to send the pictures of you
and your family. I'll put them right
next to the drawer by my bed.
Man, I'd love to hear from you.
You're still rooting for me right?
Write to me okay? Bye for now.

We Hope You Enjoyed Reading!
Let us know what you think by sending an e-mail to
editor@waterways-publishing.com

Thank You for buying **SUITCASE**. If you would like more information about waterways publishing, please join our mailing list online at **www.waterways-publishing.com**.

Visit our other imprints online:

mouthmark *(poetry)*
www.flippedeye.net/mouthmark

lubin & kleyner *(fiction)*
www.flippedeye.net/lubinandkleyner

flipped eye *(general)*
www.flippedeye.net